B

alexei biryukoff

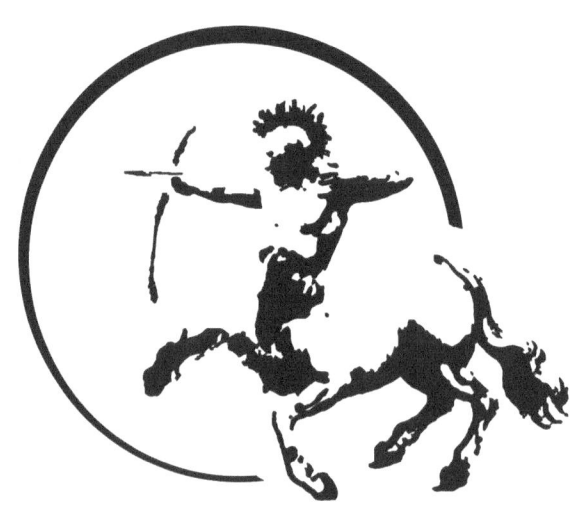

BLACK CENTAUR INC

www.blackcentaur.net

Thank You!

I would like to thank everyone in my life that has encouraged supported and inspired me. I would also like to thank those who told me that being an artist is not a career, those are the individuals who made my resolve to work hard even stronger.

"And, when you want something, all the universe conspires in helping you to achieve it."

— Paulo Coelho, The Alchemist

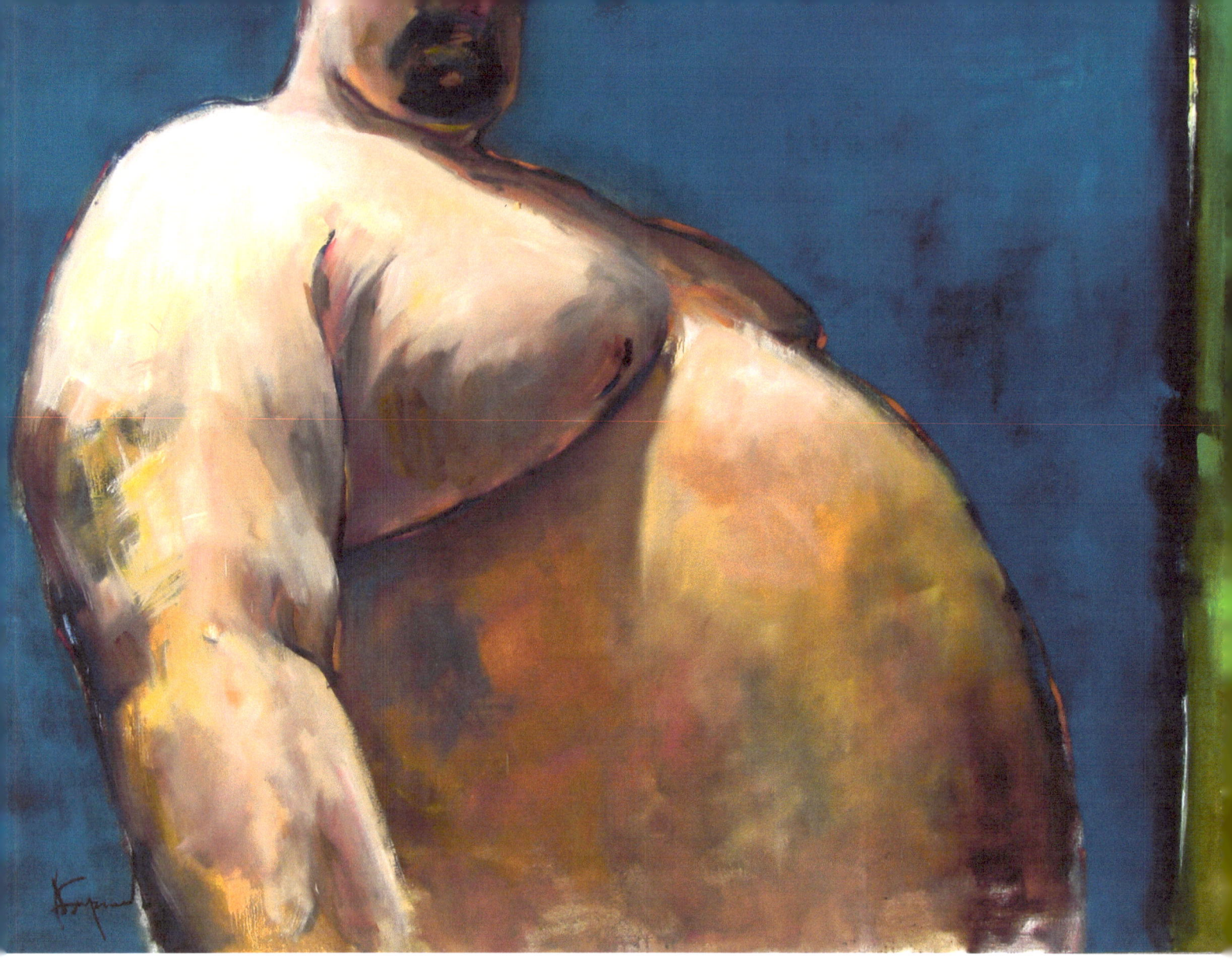

belly with a green margin   2007
oil on canvas 60x80 in

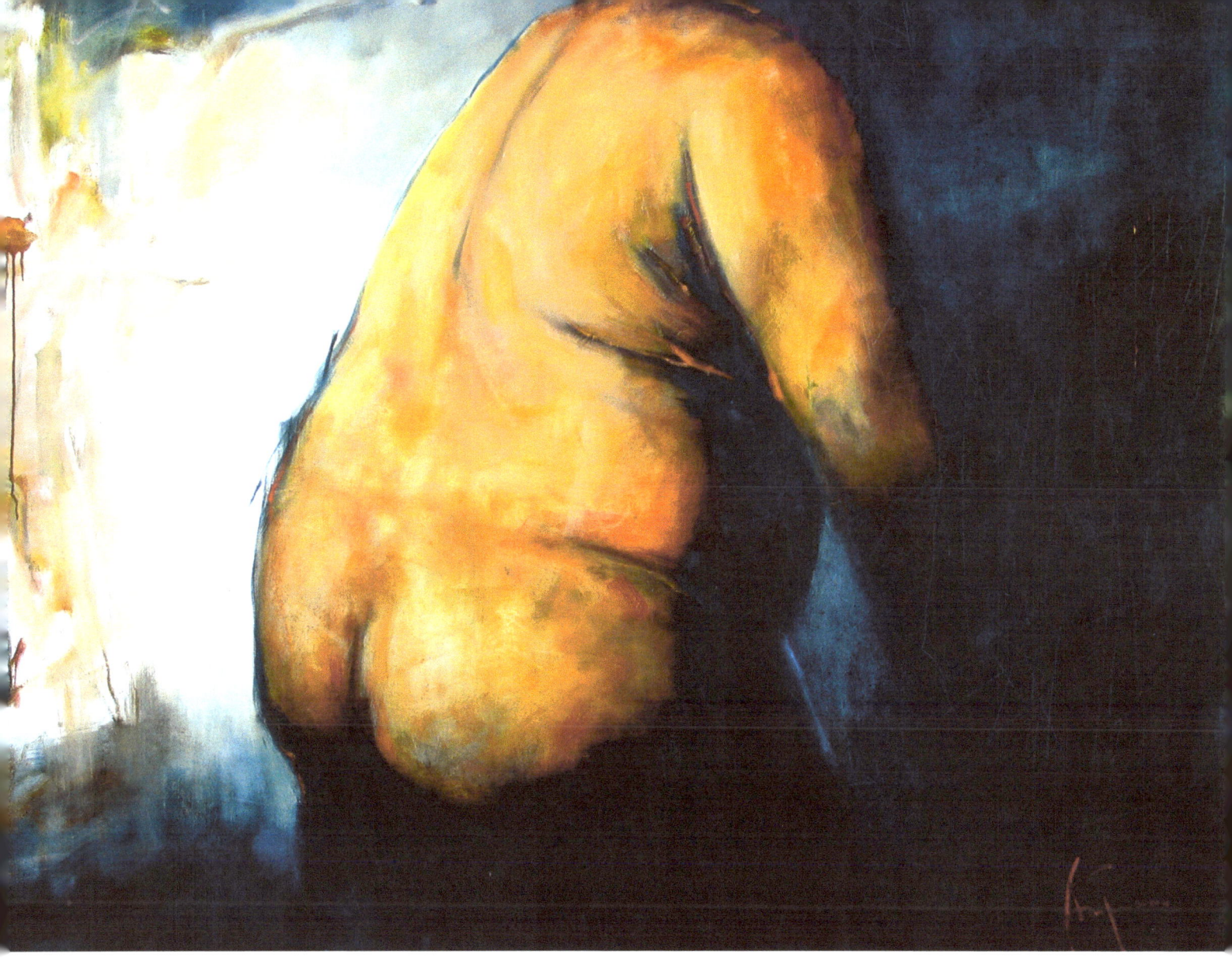

back on the black   2006
oil on canvas 60x80 in

Belief

"A state or habit of mind in which trust or confidence is placed in some person or something."

My belief is that art is a game, with no restrictions or rules to play. Just play away and enjoy the freedom. Make your every step an act of art, make people see the beauty of ordinary things, be serious, play, then mix it all up and see if anybody understands what you are doing...

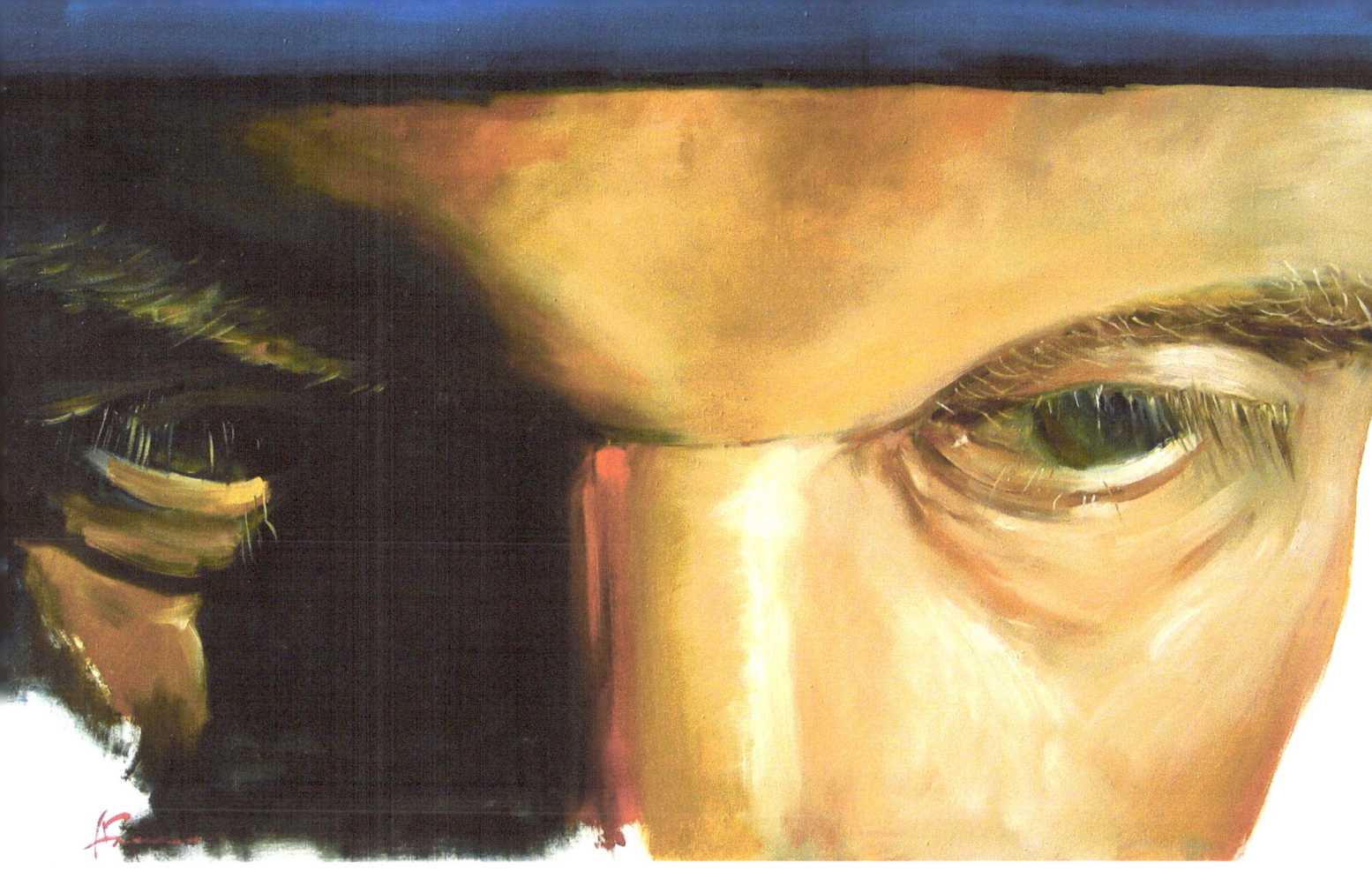

eyes   2004
oil on canvas 48x72 in

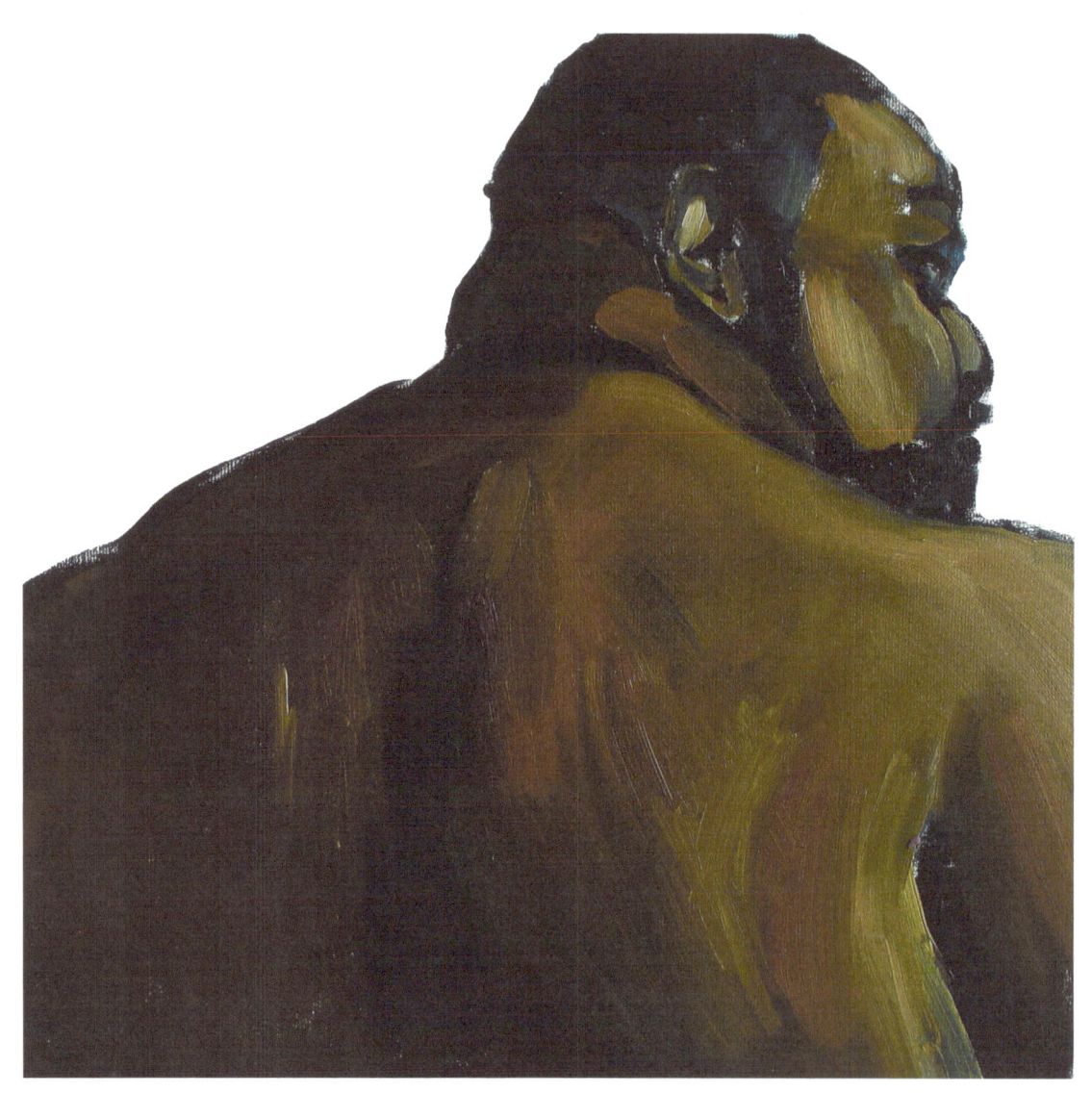

a huge fella   2008
oil on canvas 16x16 in

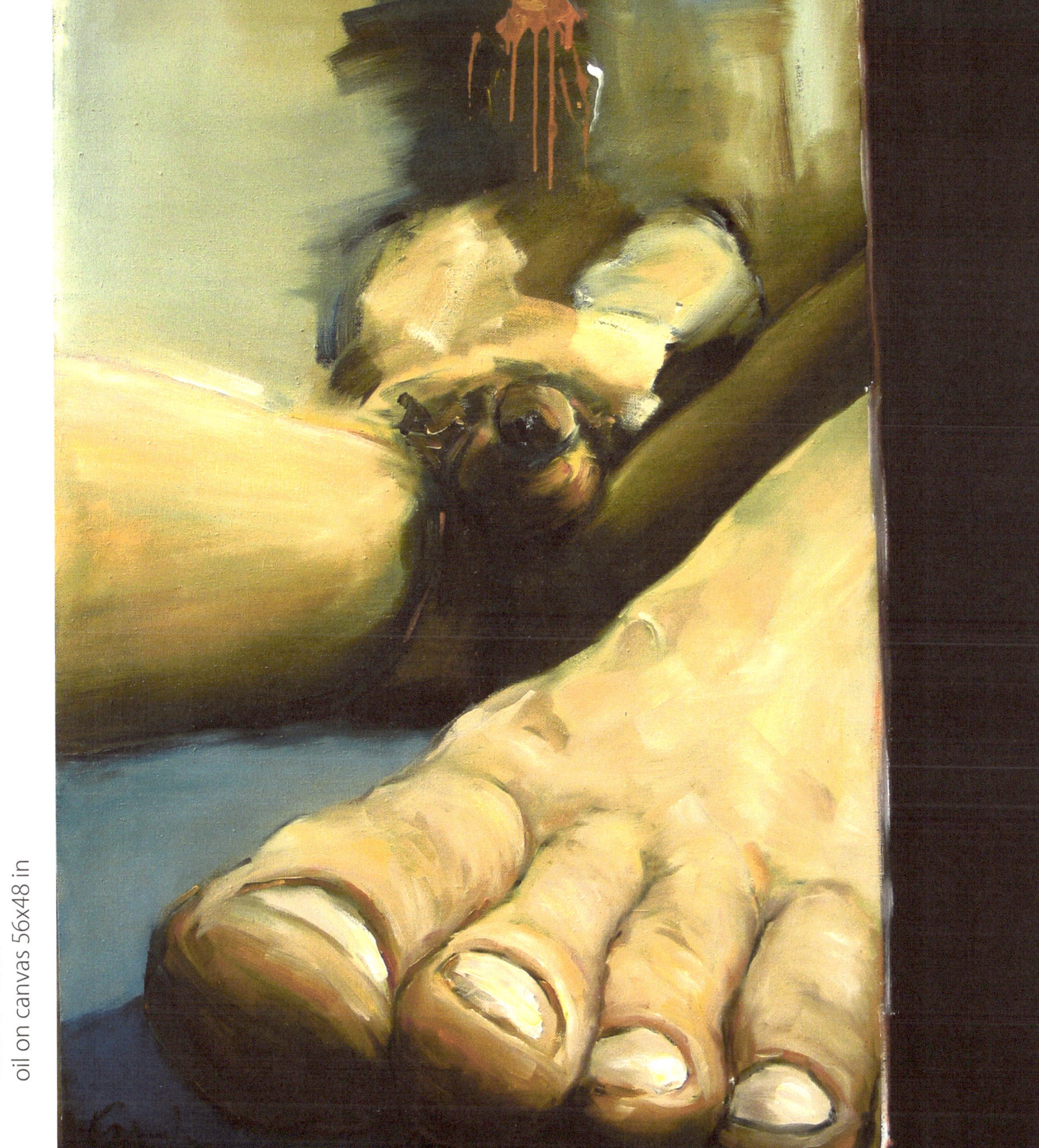

nude 3 2003
oil on canvas 56x48 in

Bones

I never set out, nor was it my intention to create "gay" art or even erotic art. My work is about the raw, masculine, natural beauty of the male form. Despite decades of progress, in modern society male nudity still carries a certain taboo and embarrassment. In many cases males in most areas of media are censored out, or if given any attention it is only from behind. The raw masculine form has been replaced by over-retouched magazine covers, making the average joe try to live up to an unrealistic body image, but this is not new - women have been dealing with this issue for many years.

Beauty, of course, is in the eyes of the beholder. But lines, curves and textures of the male leave a great deal open for the viewer to interpret and see from their own reference point.

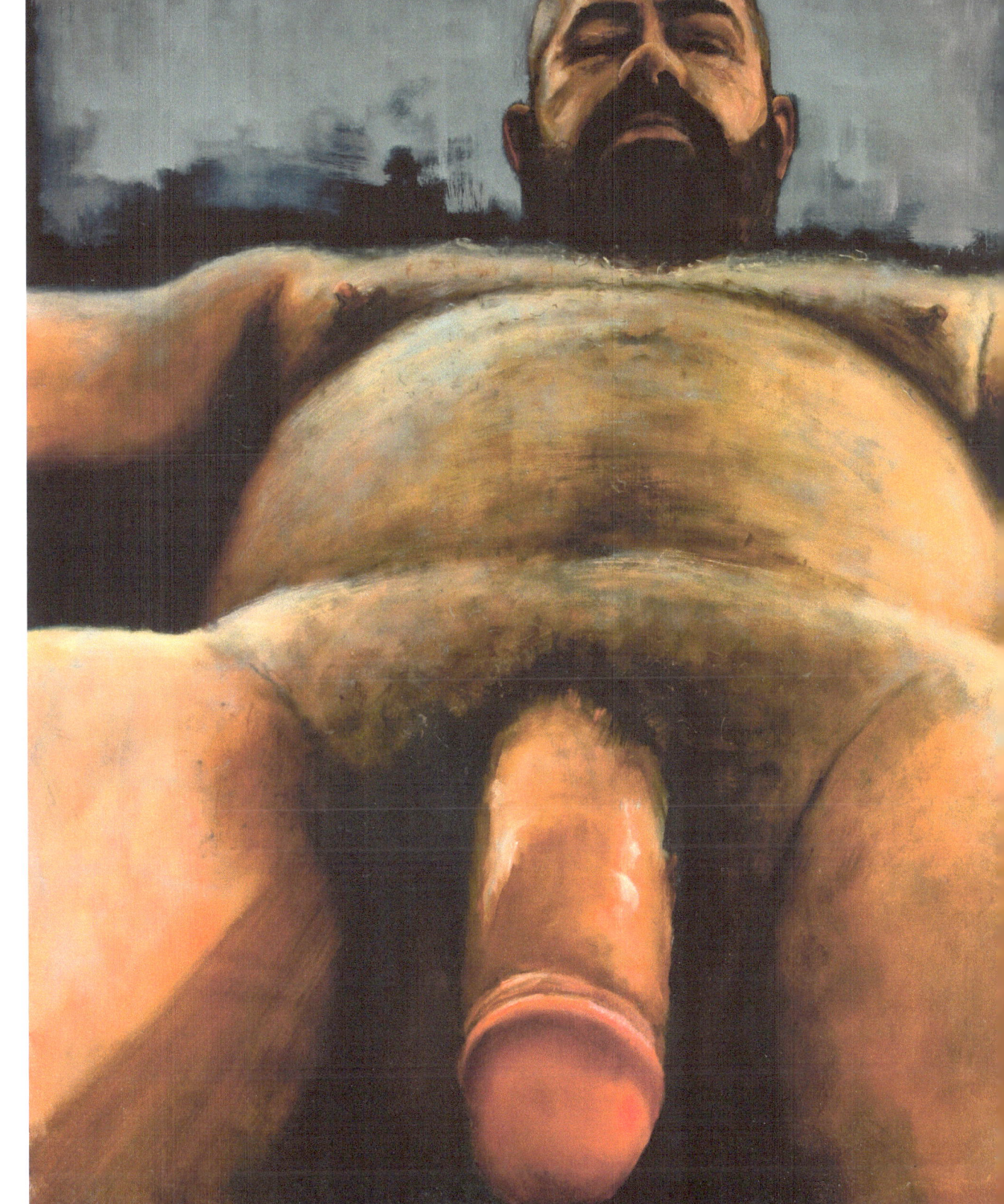

Mack 2012
oil on canvas 59x48 in

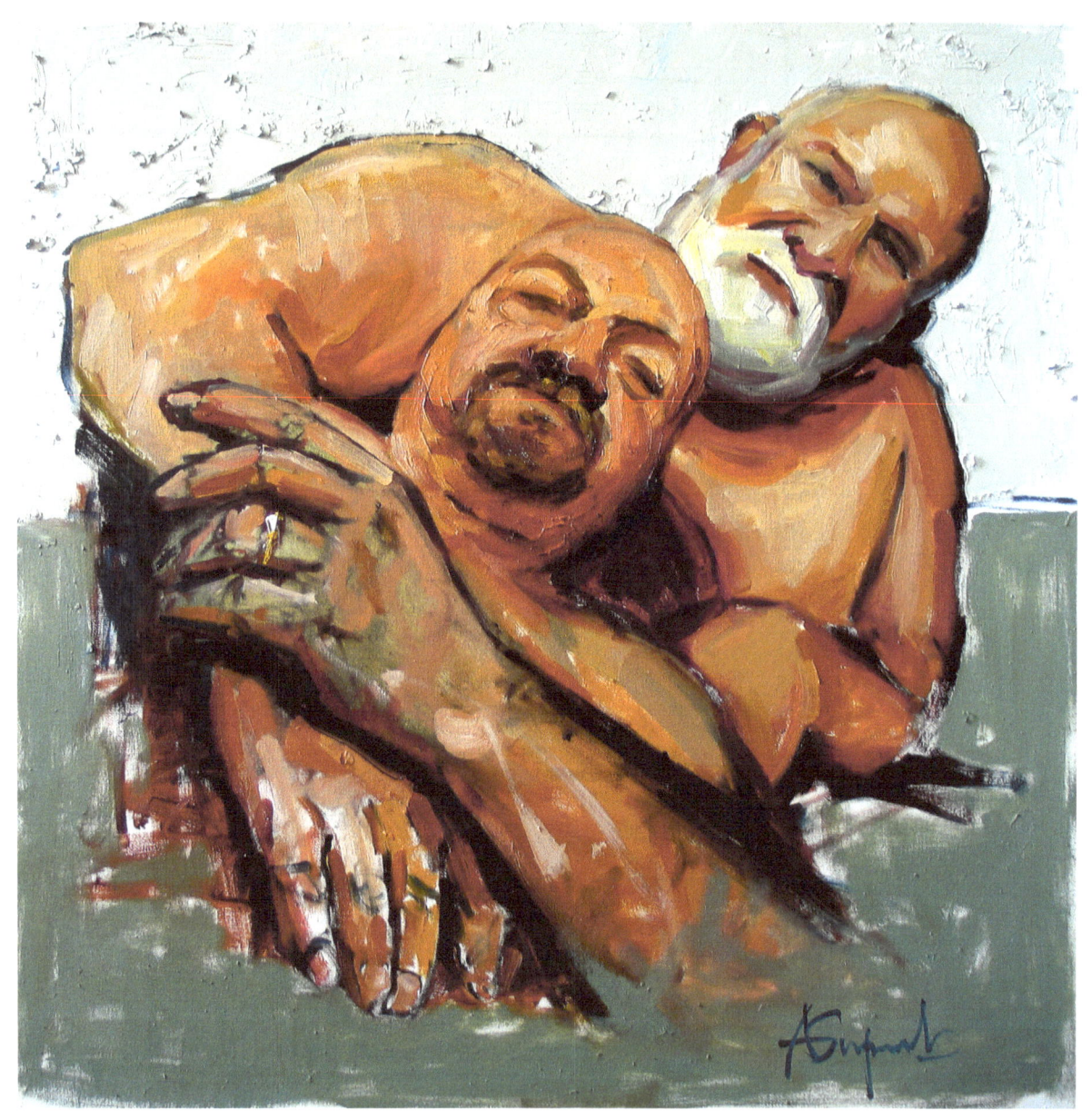

Bruce and Warren 2009
oil on canvas 24x24 in

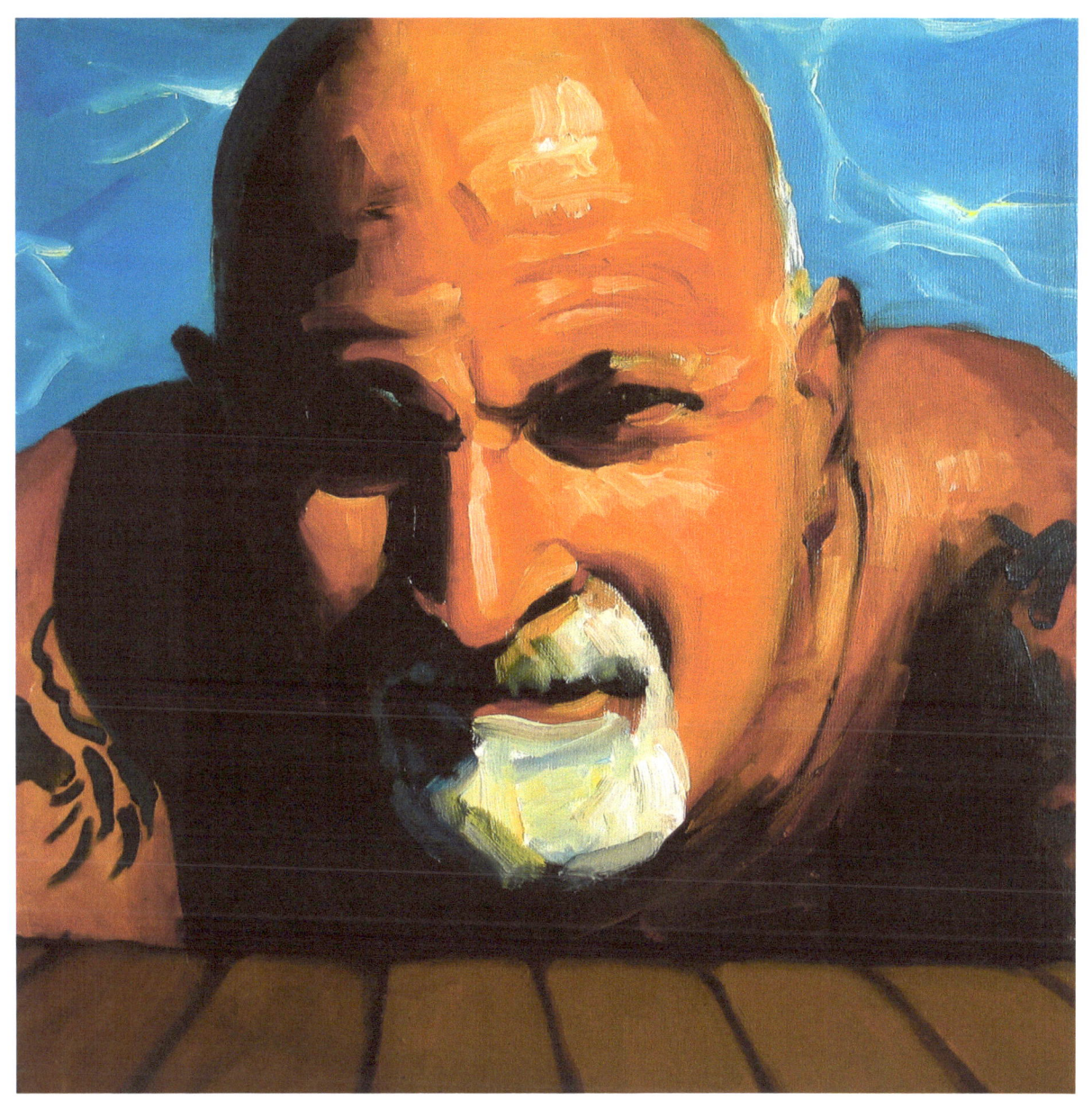

in the pool 1   2008
oil on canvas 16x16 in

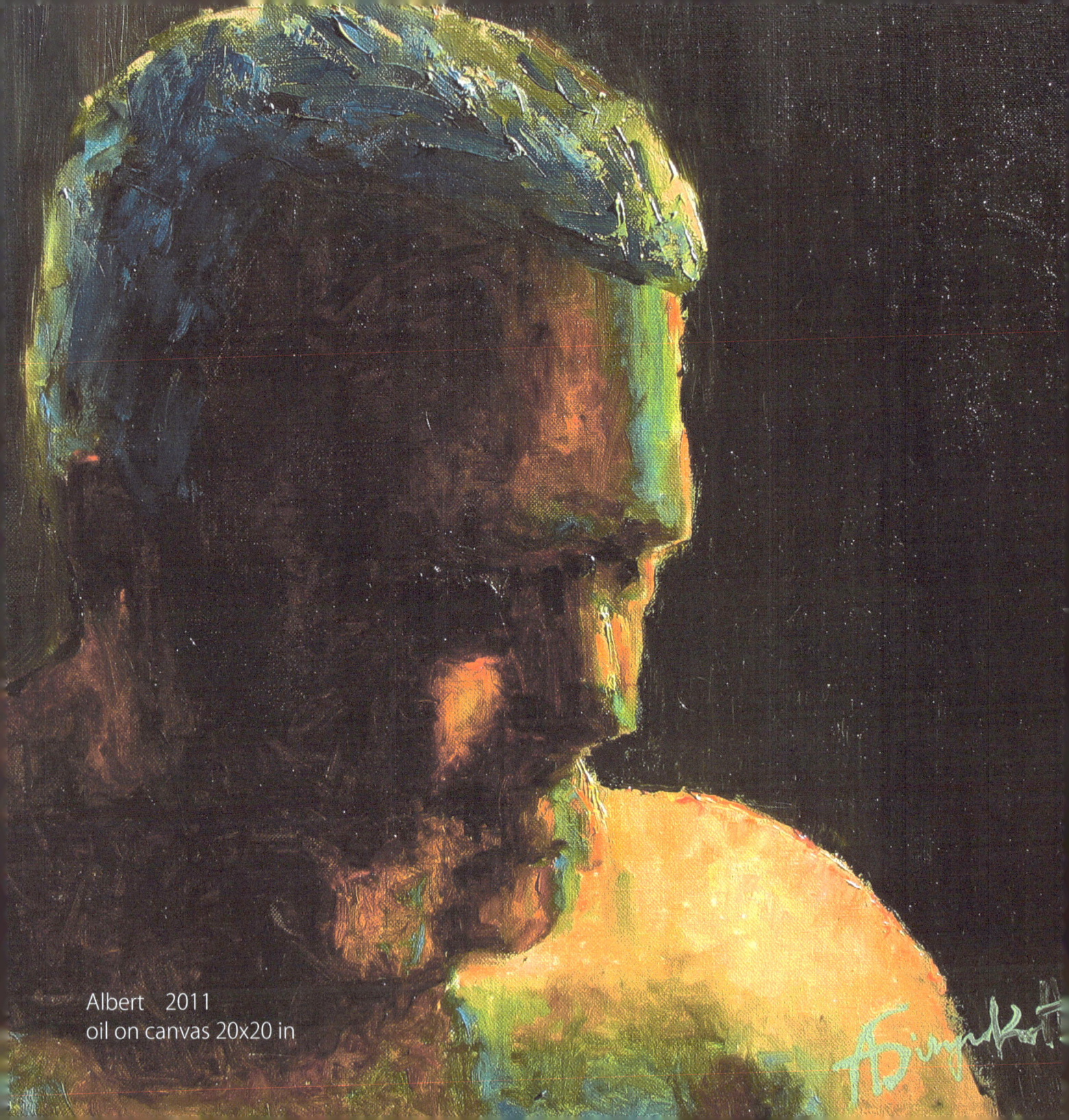

Albert   2011
oil on canvas 20x20 in

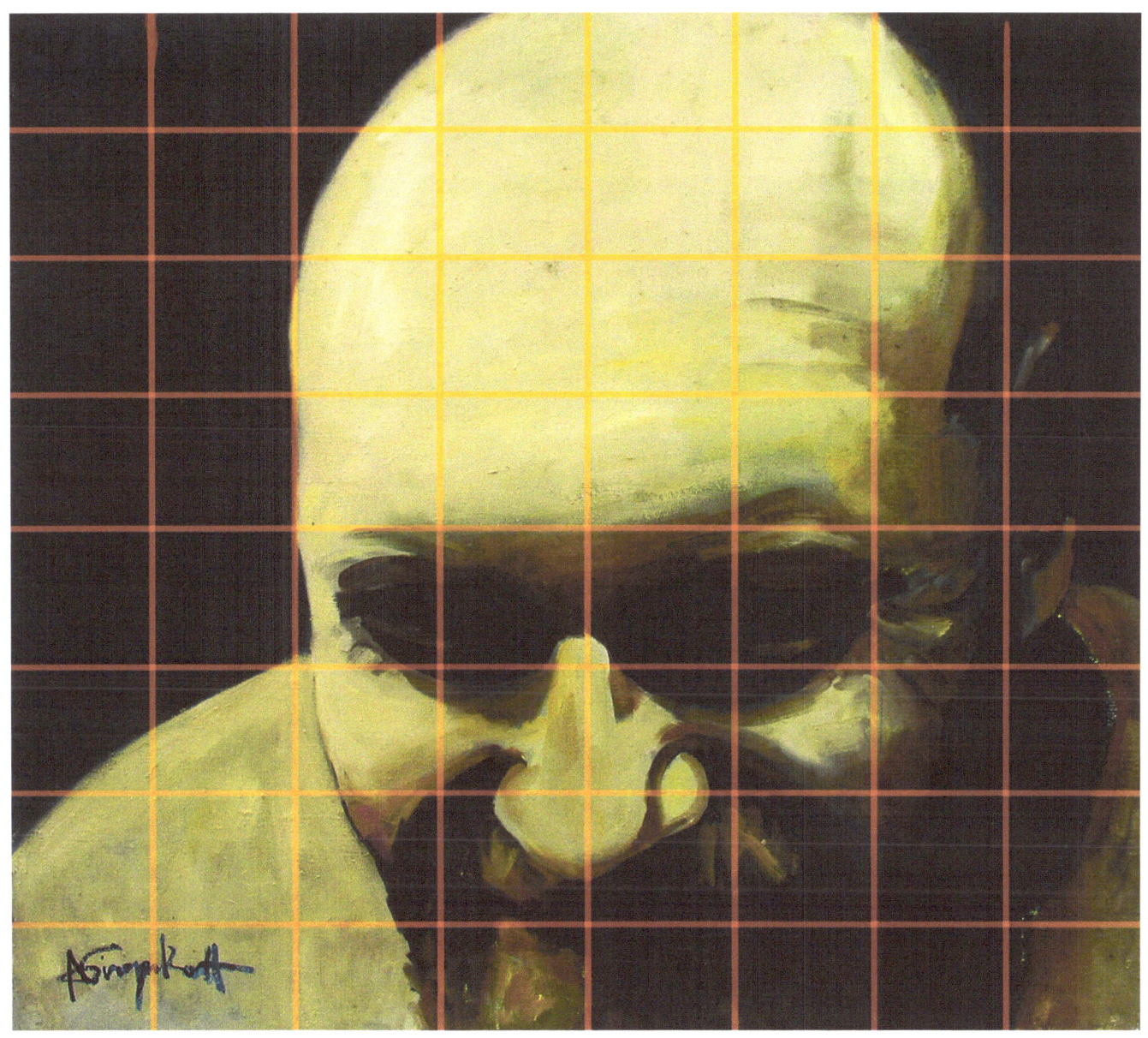

Thomas 2010
oil on canvas 32x32 in

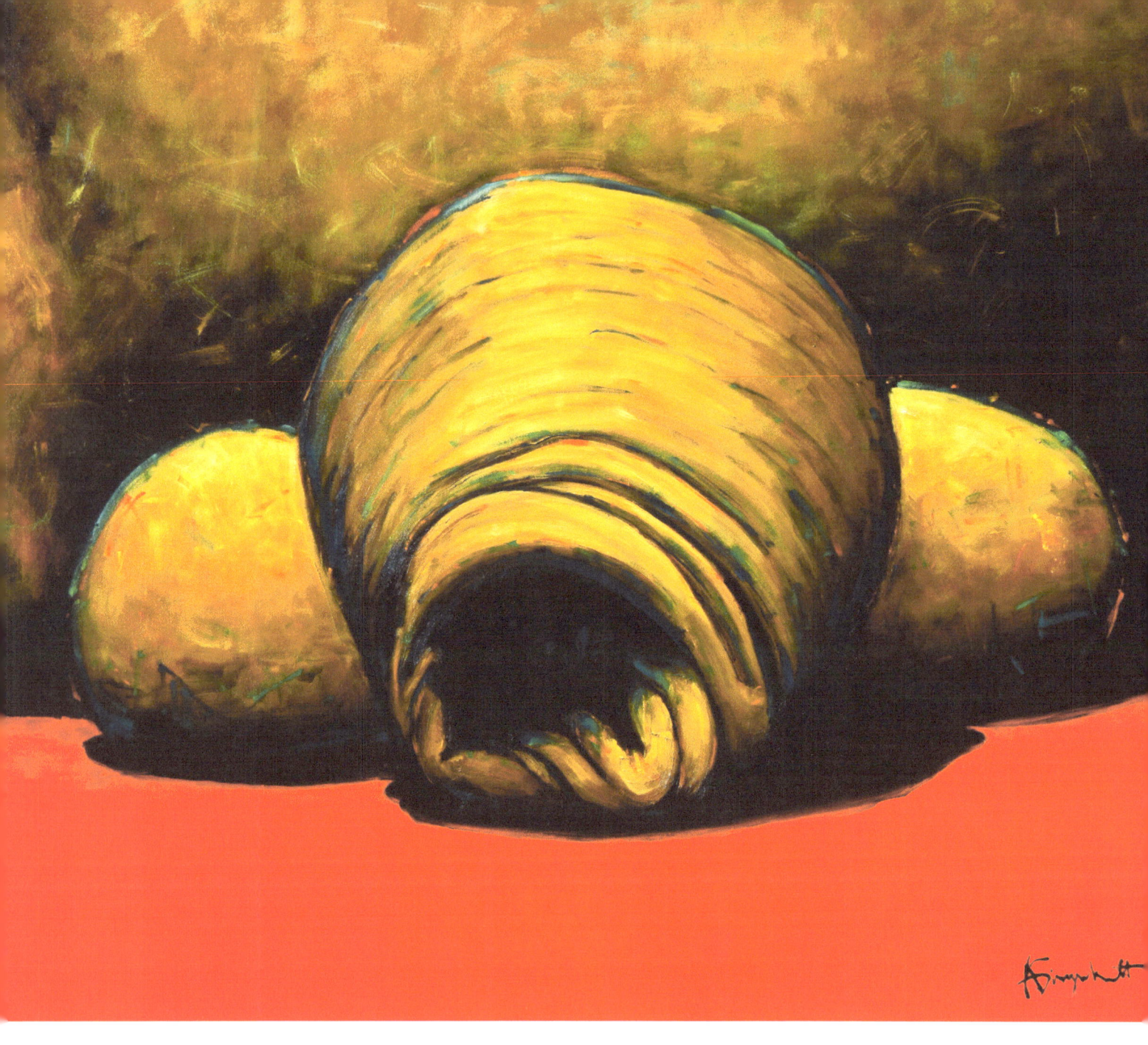

manhood 2011
oil on canvas 48x60 in

Barnaul

Siberian wasteland...I don't think so.

I was actually born in Soviet warm Arizona-like Kyrgyzstan, then became a pioneer in Kazakhstan where I reached sexual maturity, then moved to Barnaul Siberia where I watched the iron curtain fall and all the wild changes that followed the Perestroyka era - the rise of the Russian mafia with their Bentleys, scarlet velvet suits and huge crosses on thick gold chains (which apparently makes us the most orthodox god chosen people...I guess), first cell phones, dial-up internet, private businesses, imported crap from cheap markets of Poland and China, McDonalds, first travel agencies taking you outside of Russia, food rationing stamps, legal rock concerts, $150 fake 501's and Sega games... It was CRAZY !

I was asked once how it feels to live in Siberia and this was my response:
"It feels like you are in an expensive cultural butt hole, stuck in your room with double insulated windows from October till the end of April.
The upside of this experience is that you can appreciate the advantages of other places, cause you know the difference... Seeing homeless people in New York sitting on the sidewalk, wearing white socks and 100 dollar boots, makes you wonder why people can't appreciate all the opportunities laying right at their feet and just choose to be bums, some I agree can't help their situation but many can if they choose...

Барнаул

Siberia is not a bad place to live after all, the worst thing I disliked there is that everything seems to be a copy or stylization of what you see in Hollywood movies (which by itself is a total crap to me) but when it turns into a pretence imitation, it is even worse...

The good side of life there is that you still can get some good homemade natural food vs. pre-chewed over-flavored processed biomass - western "civilized" food to me tastes like plastic. In Siberia you can go wherever you like, put up a tent and make a camp fire without any permits or fear that you are trespassing on someone's property... there is a lot of rugged freedom there that I really miss."
After all this is where my art tastes and work were shaped.

Now I am here in the US, and I must admit it has been an adjustment, but at least it's not -40 Celsius. I actually am enjoying my time here in the USA.

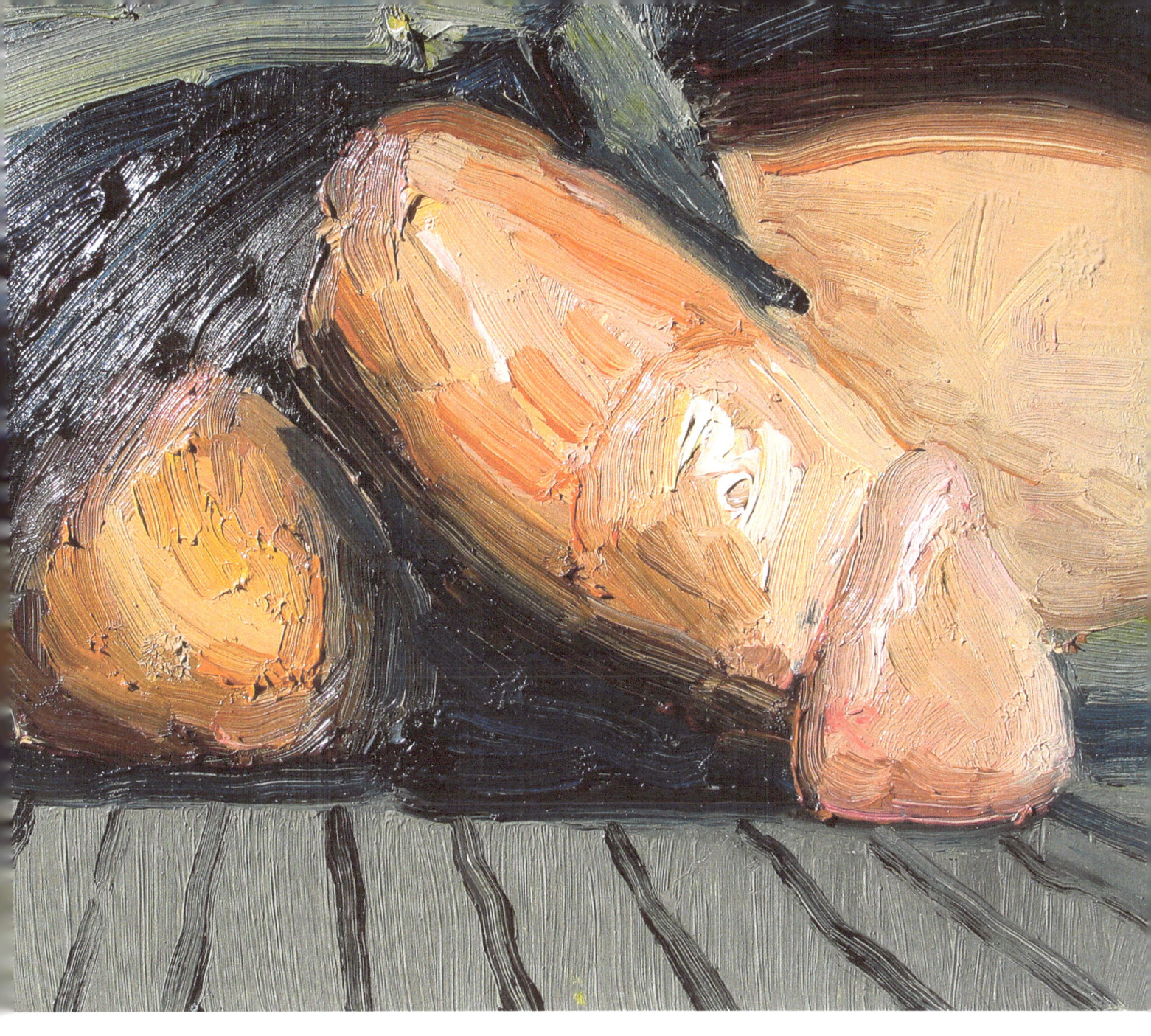

tbone   2012
oil on cardboard 5x6 in

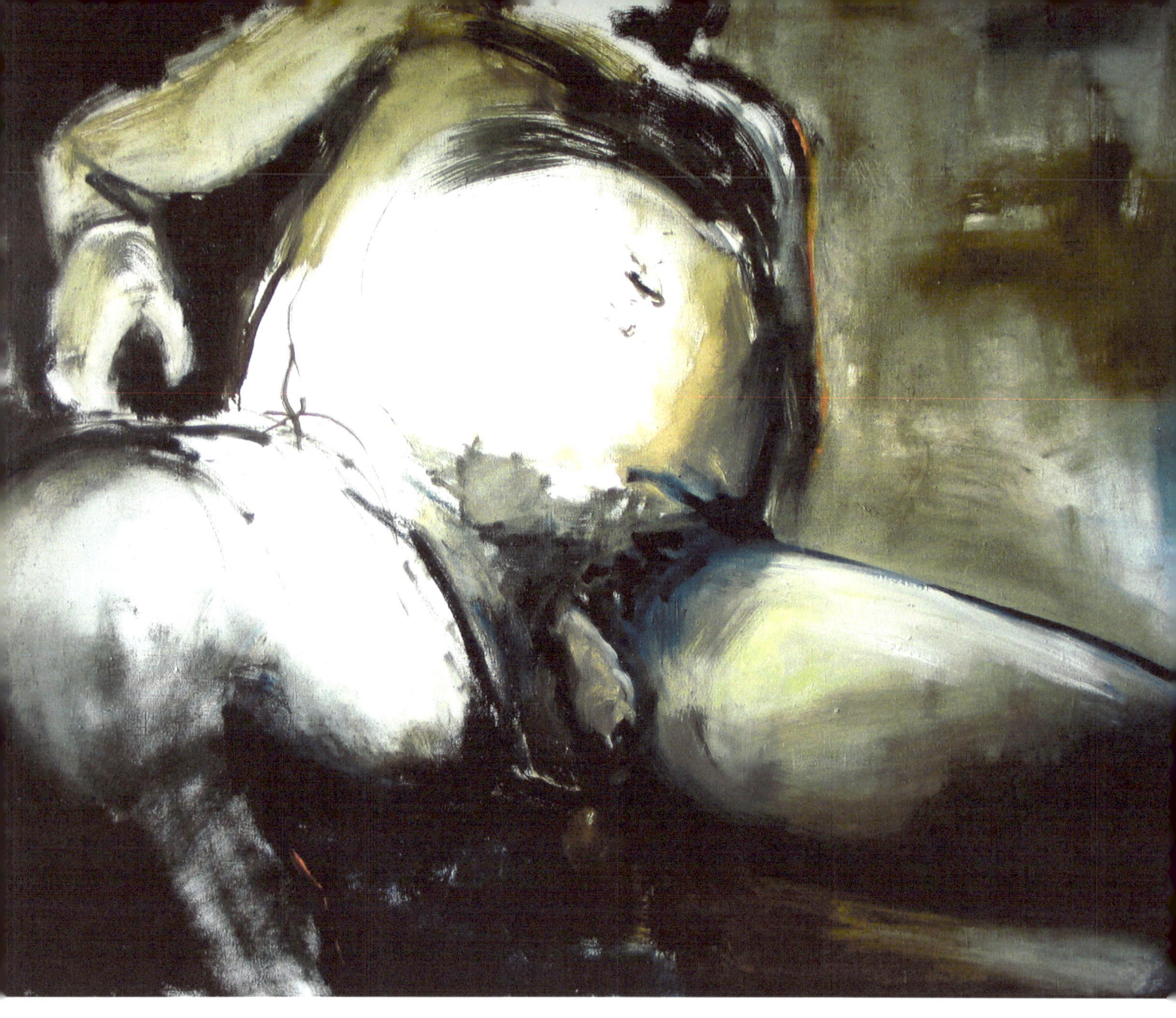

nude 10   2005
oil on canvas 52x60 in

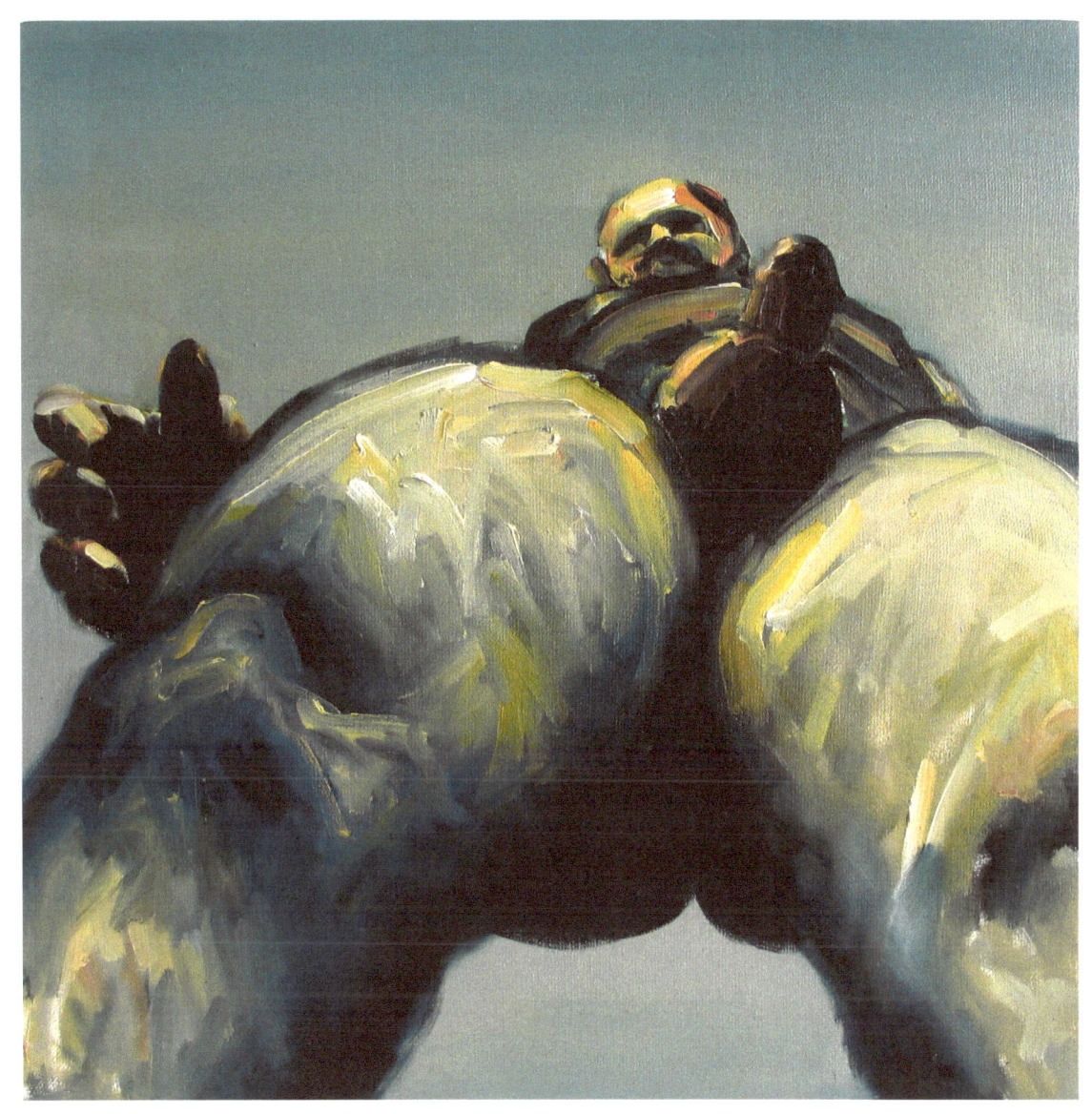

spanish view   2008
oil on canvas 16x16 in

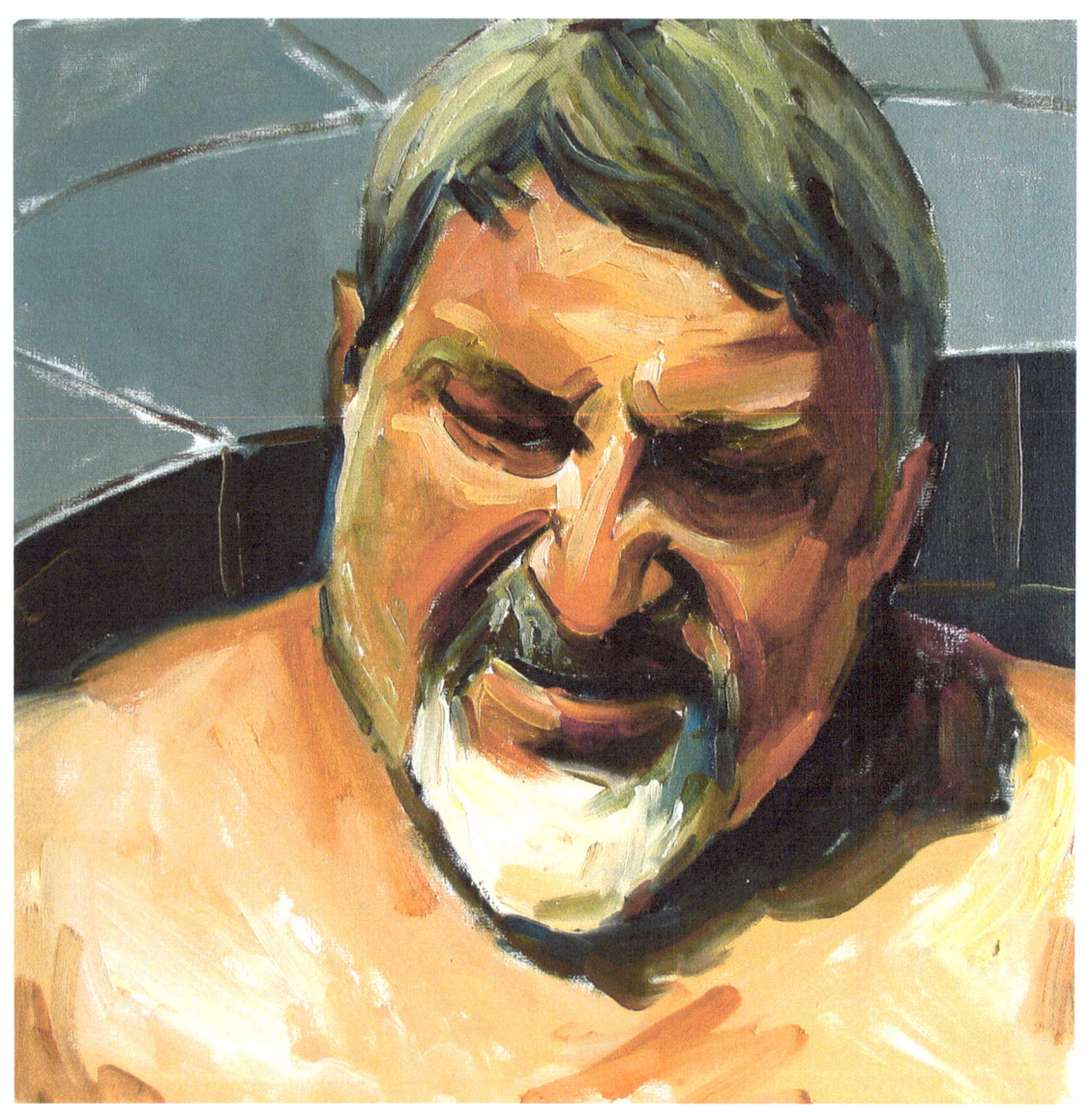

in the pool 2   2008
oil on canvas 16x16 in

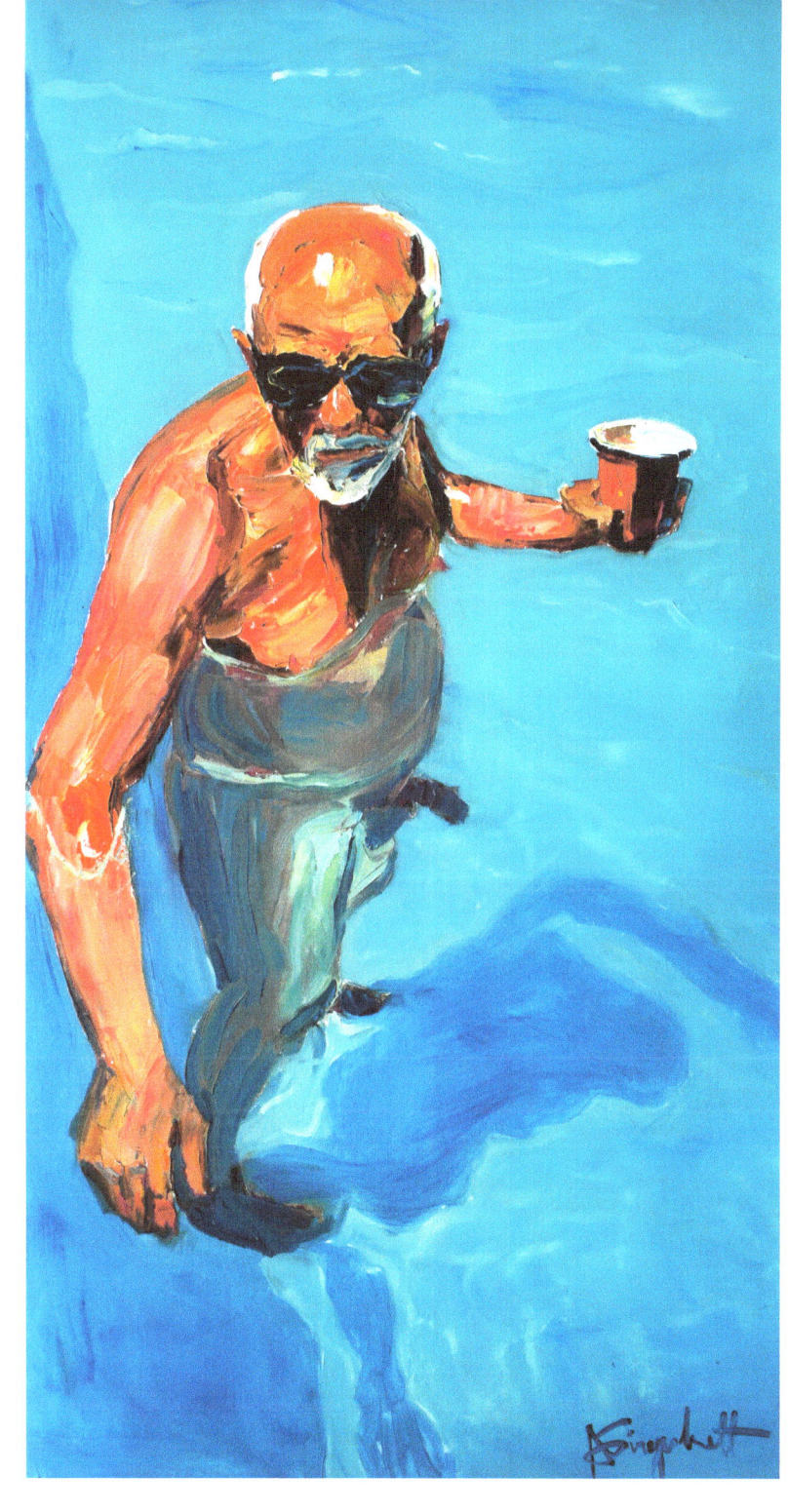

an old man with a drink   2011
oil on canvas 48x24 in

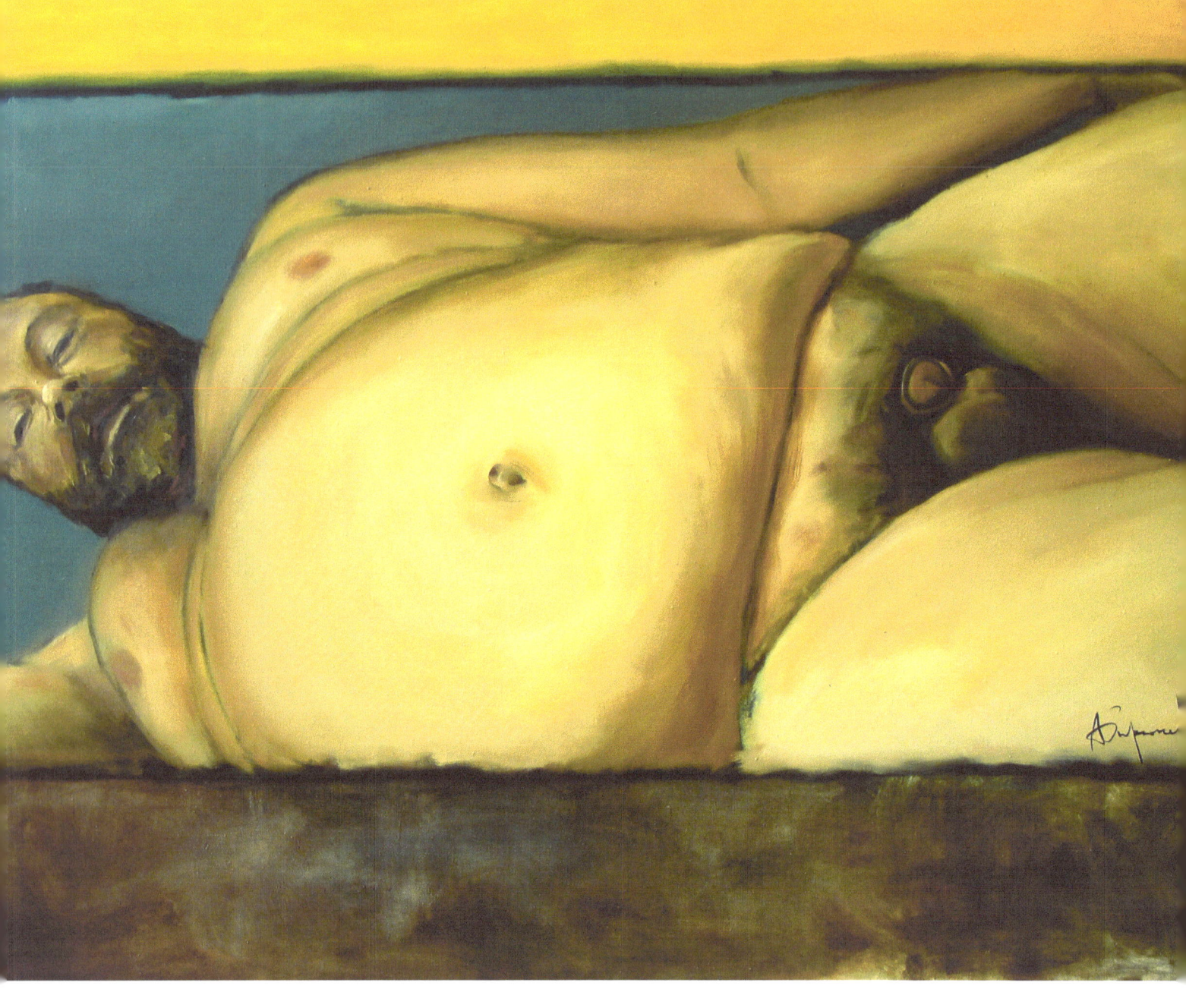

nude 5 2004
oil on canvas 64x80 in

Harlan 2007 »
oil on canvas 60x60 in

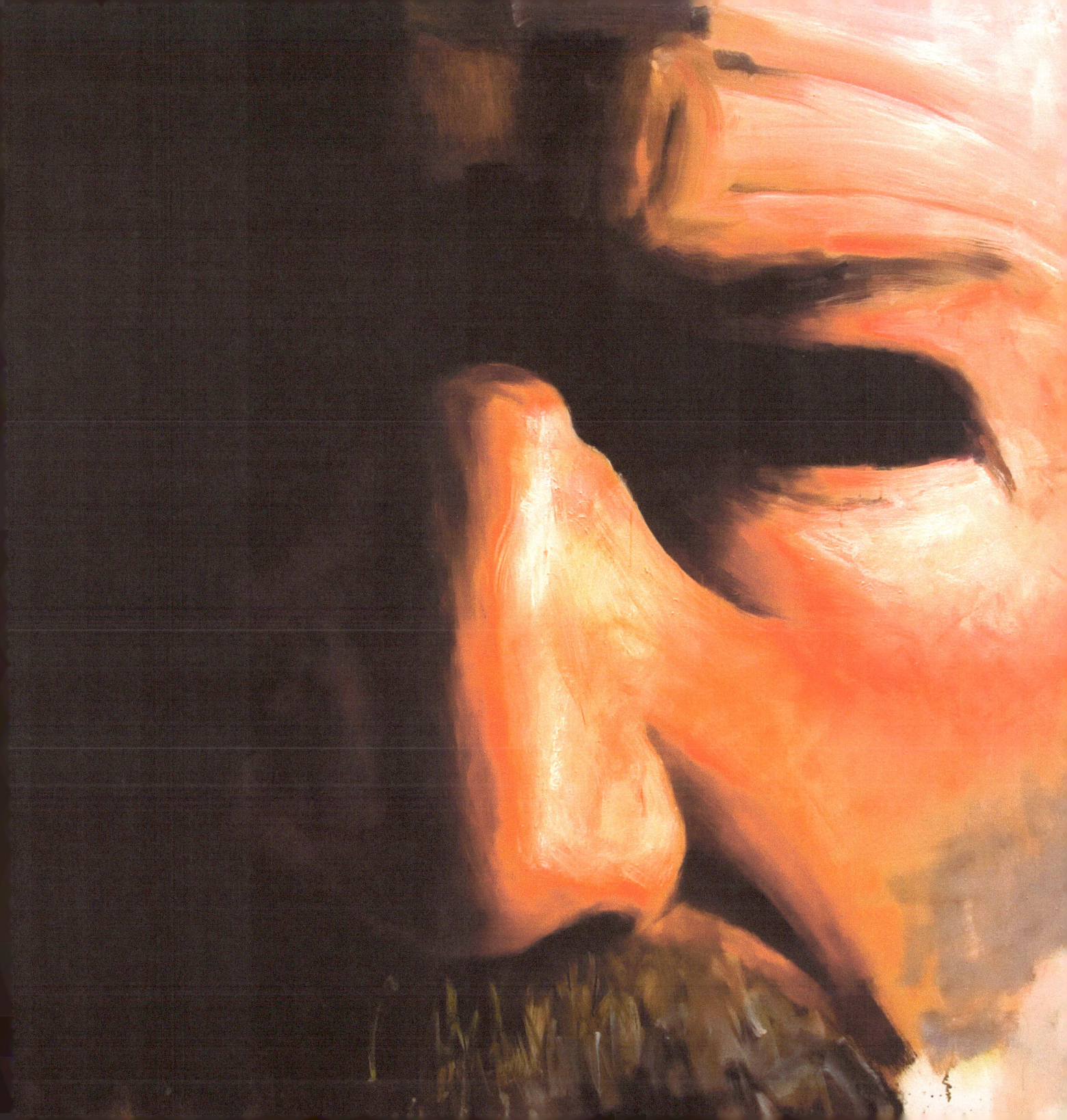

Yes you can sometimes see balls in my works but I don't only paint them. Having balls is not easy at times...

On Apil 14th 2004 in Barnaul I put on a joint show with a friend of mine in the only contemporary gallery in this Siberian town of 800 thousand people. A week later we were ordered by the local authorities to shut down or be arrested due to my painting Nude #2, because it showed a bold 5x5 ft close up of a man's crotch. My partner's work showed boobs and bush, and that was ok, but ball sack and cock were considered porn by the Barnaul Ministry of Culture.
Nude #2 earned the nick name "2 heads".
2 years later it traveled 5800 miles to Cedar Rapids Iowa (yes Iowa) to take part in a group show called Uncovered. It then mysteriously vanished somewhere between Colorado and New Mexico, along with a couple of other works...so to make a long story short I don't know where my balls are...
but if you see them please let me know, I miss them...

Balls

nude 2 2003   »
oil on canvas 60x60 in

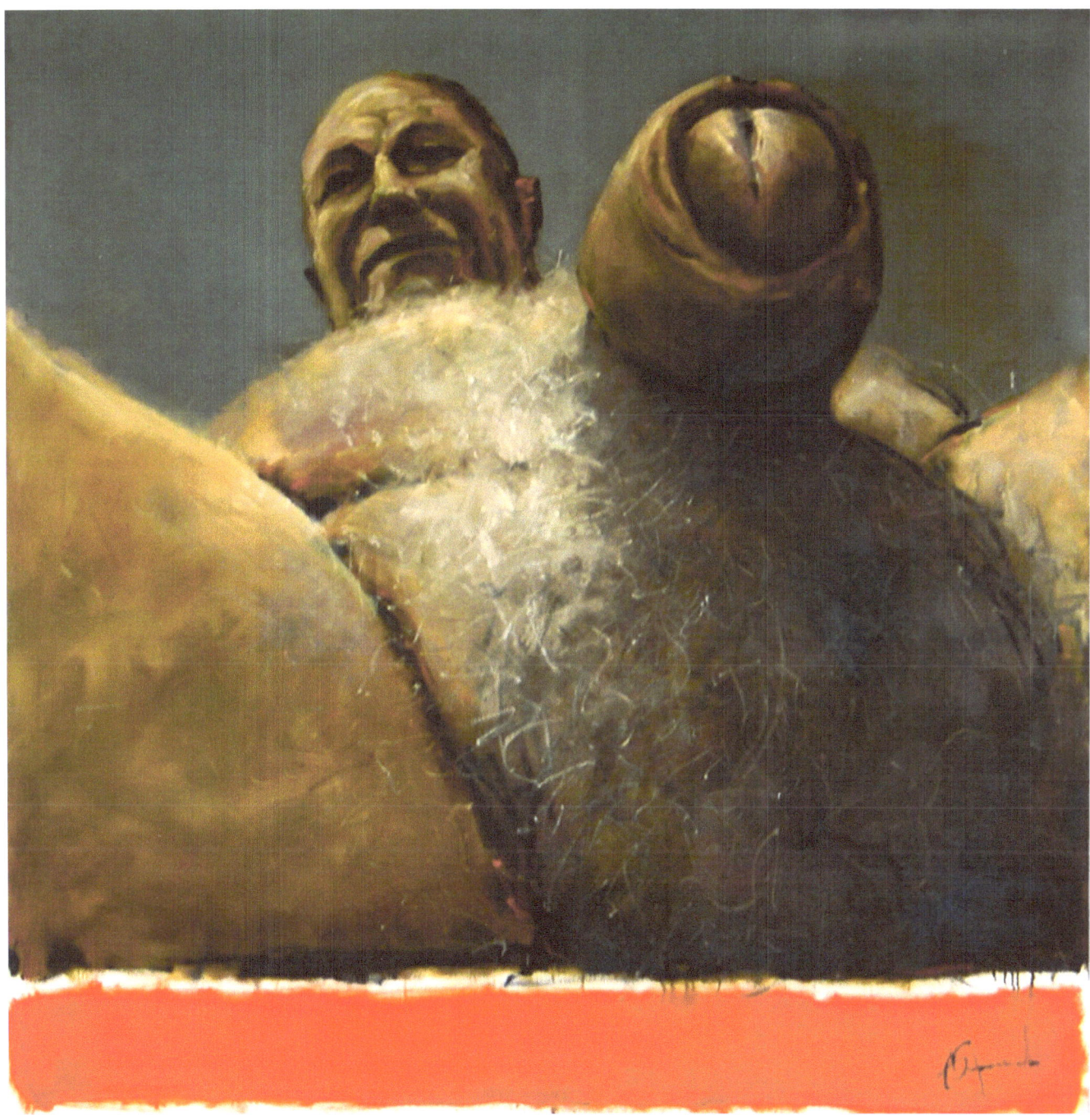

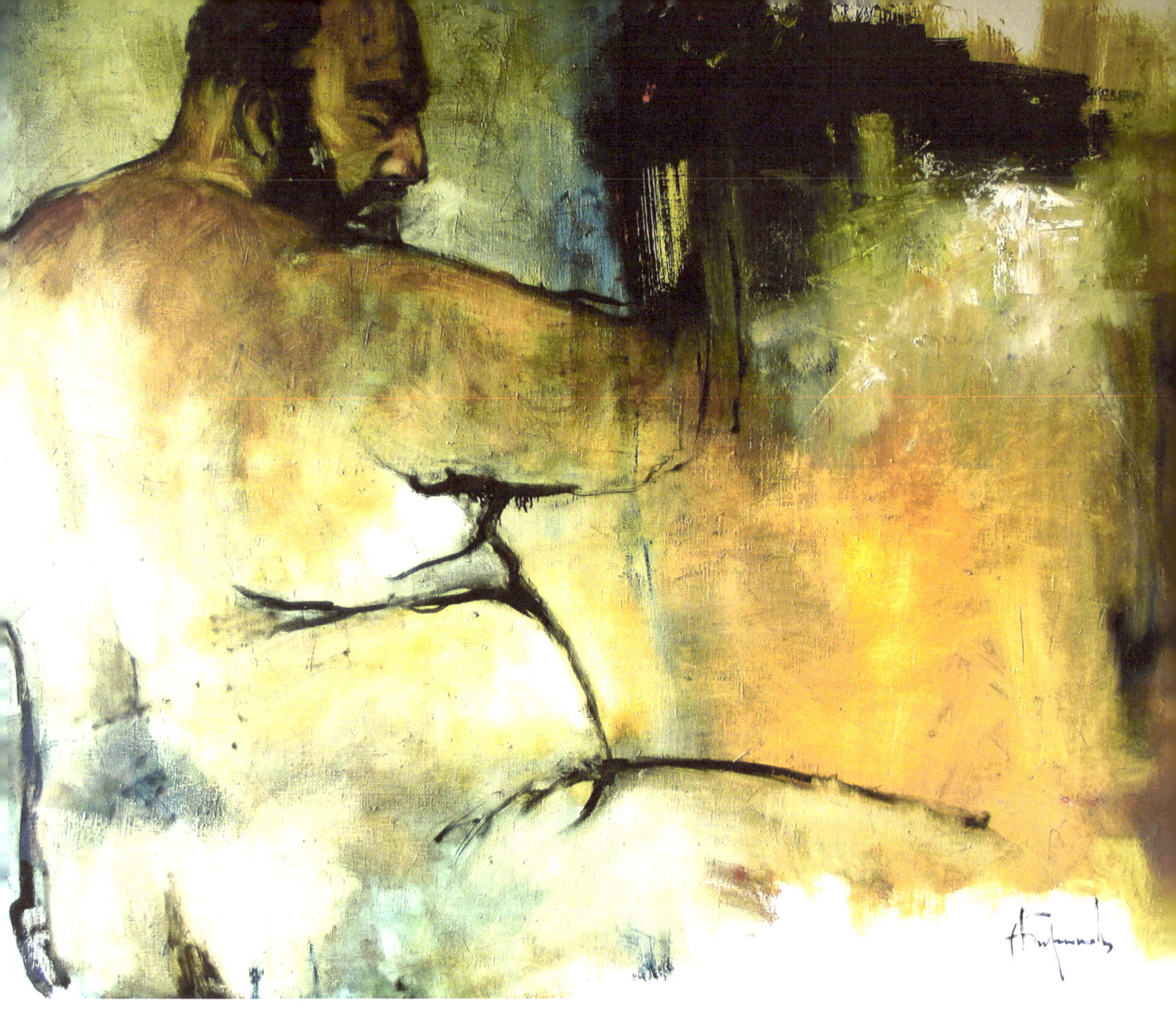

nude 8 2005
oil on canvas 52x64 in

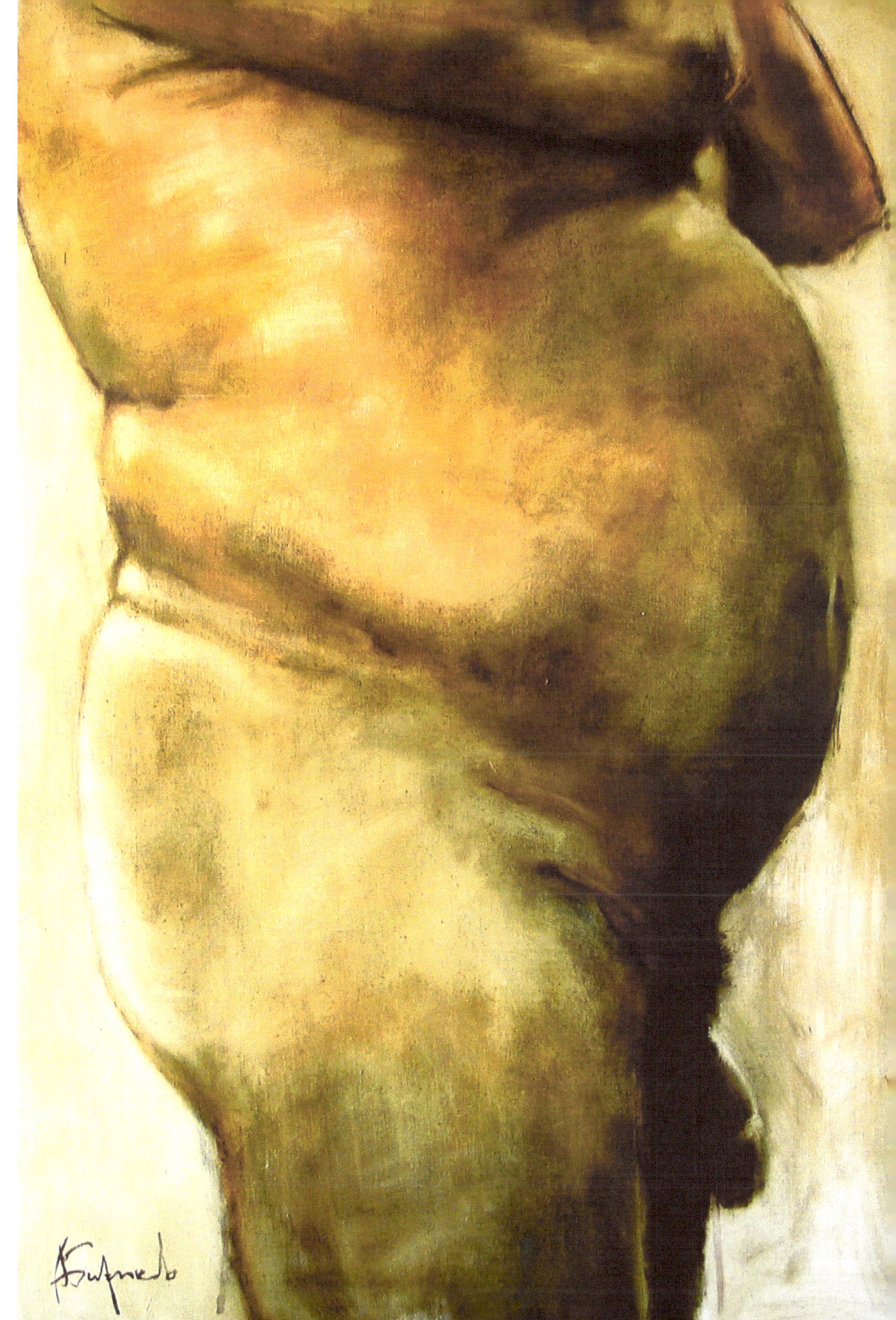

nude 12   2005
oil on canvas 60x40 in

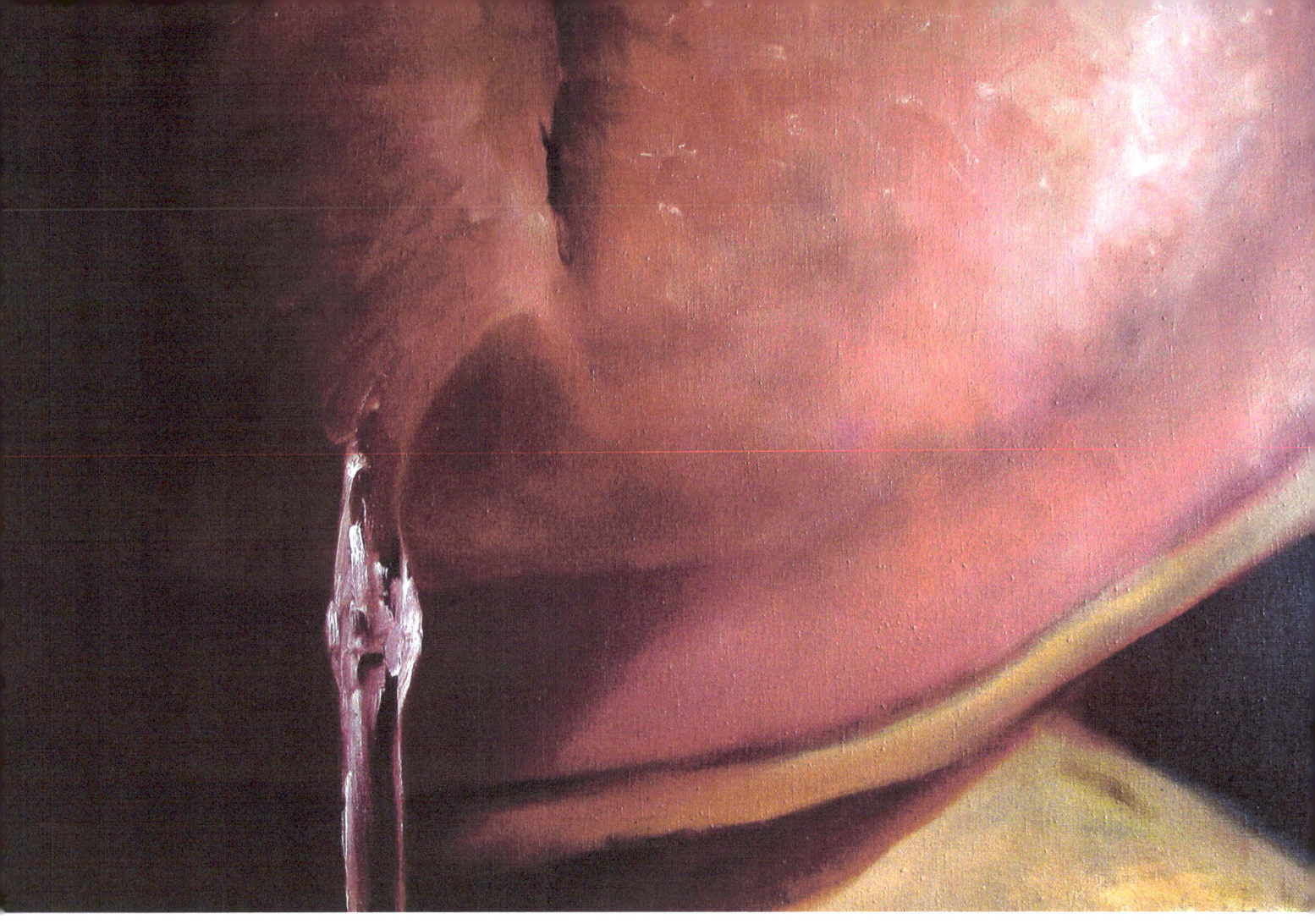

drool 2006
oil on canvas 40x60 in

Sorry guys, but I have to tell the truth here, so if some of the ladies
 see this, they are just going to have to understand.
As males we do look at other men, maybe not in a sexual way
but we do look! Growing up we see our older brothers or maybe our
fathers nude, and we compare our bodies to theirs, wondering:
"when it will grow"
"when will i get hair down there?"
" will mine be as big ?"
As we age we see others in the gym at school or in porno movies
and think "WOW! I wish I was hung like that…"

Men develop an appreciation of the male body. Whether it be bikers
and beer bellies, or body builders and biceps, we look at other
men and compare ourselves, and have a healthy admiration
for a bro with a bod!

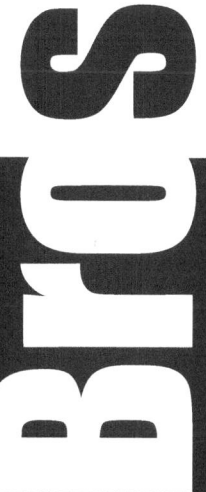

Bros

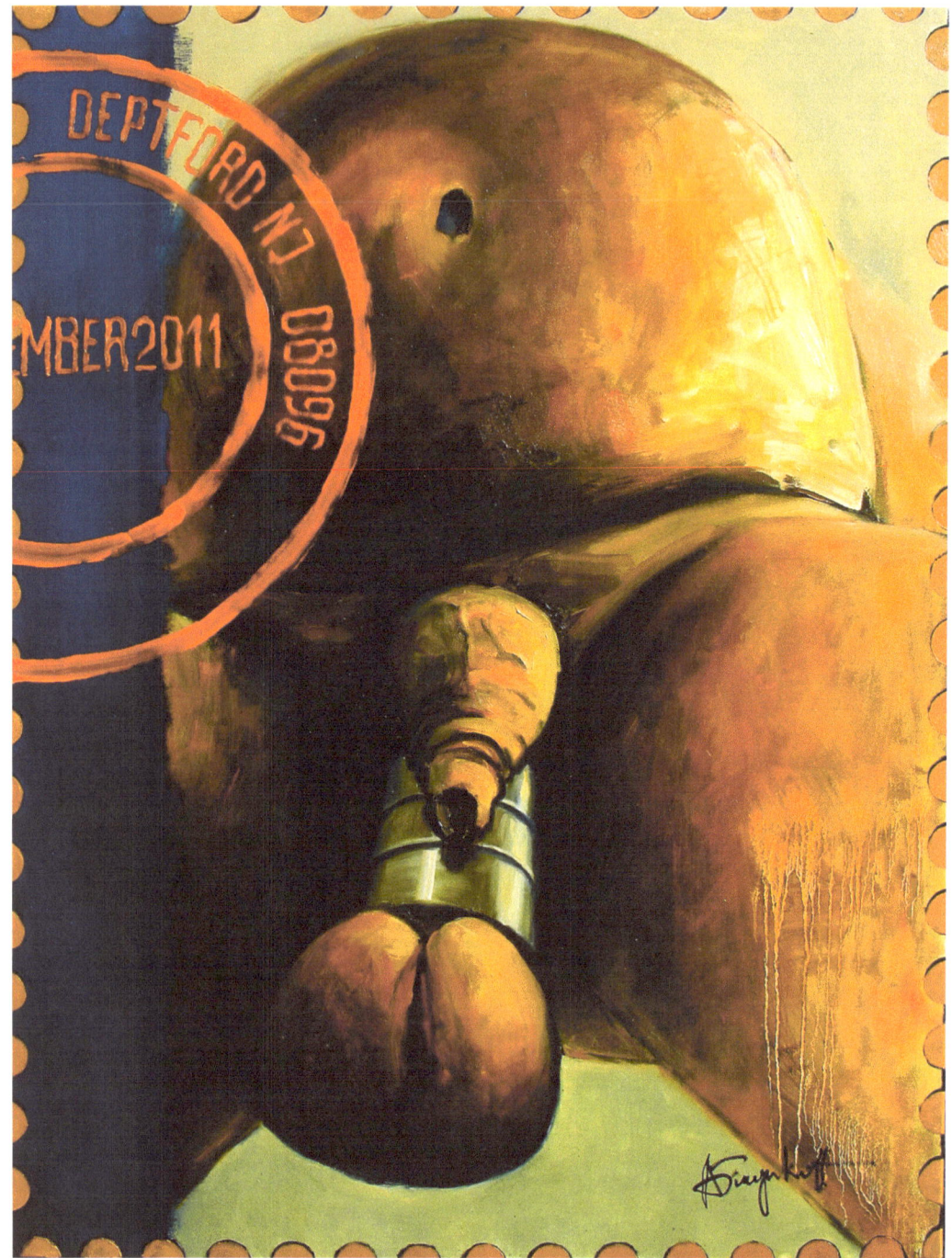

postman 2011
oil on canvas 48x36 in

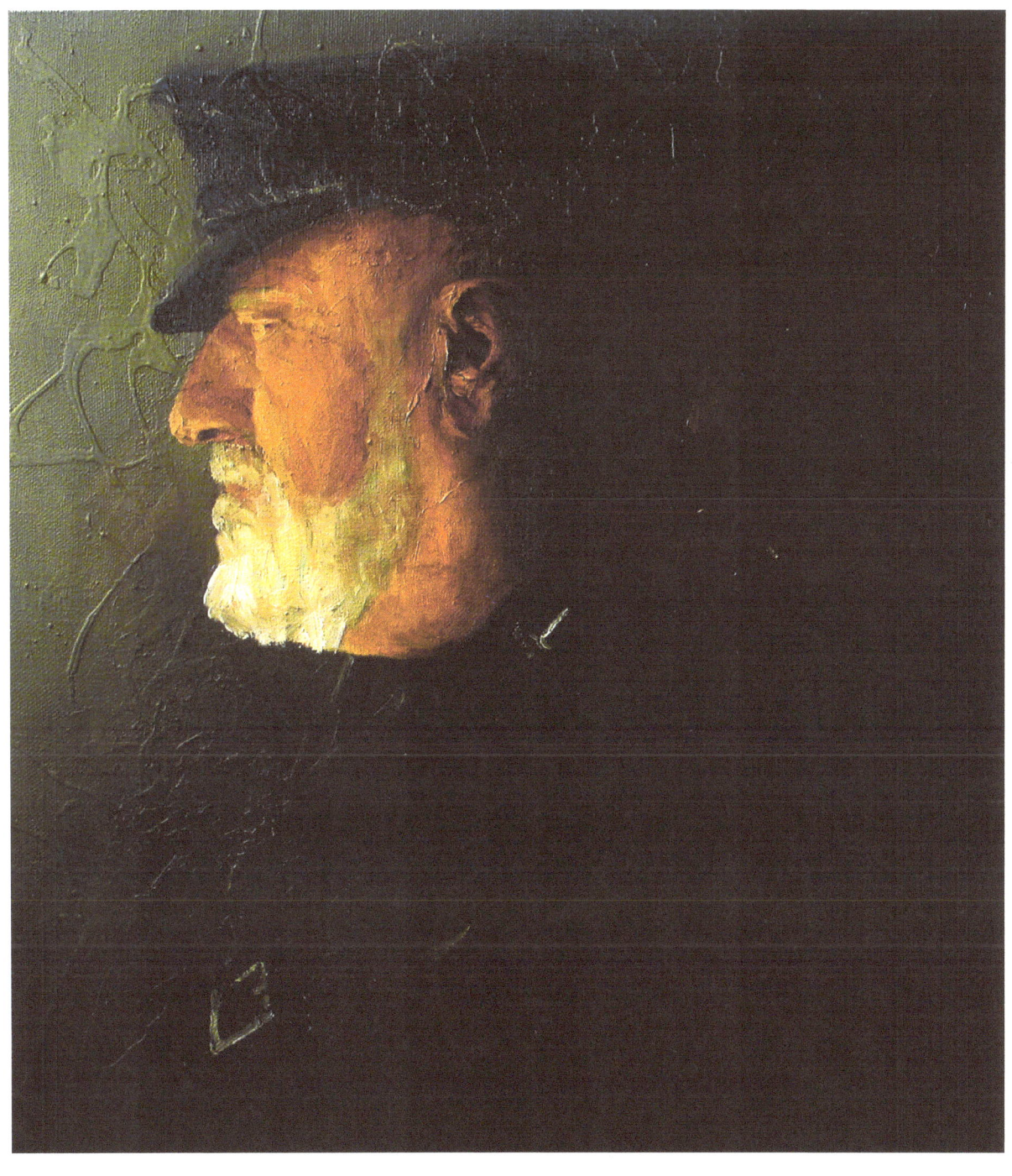

Earl Gray 2007
oil on canvas 35x30 in

I tried to come up with a "B" word that best describes me and although many of my friends had quite a few suggestions ie: ball-breaker, bastard, bitch, bumpkin, badass, etc..
they only showed pieces of me, plus I would never want to put words like that in a book...<eg>
I really liked the word borscht, because my interests are wide and varied, just like borscht is a bunch of meat and vegetables all stirred up into one tasty mess.

I have been a passionate sound artist since 2004 and love to make field recordings of everything from birds and brooks, to the buzz of construction sites and railroads, take it back to my studio and turn it into a story told with sounds that move you to a different place and time. My alter ego - the sound artist Muhmood can sometimes overtake me.

I can spend all day with a good book.. (I hope this is a good book and you will spend a day with it...or at least 15 minutes)

I love good food and love to cook it, especially good old fashioned stuff like mom makes, like borscht, and blini, and beet root salad, and the occasional vodka shots with pickles is a great way to spend time with good friends.

I'm a shutter bug, I'll admit it. I pretty much have my camera with me all the time and a few times I was told I have a serious photographic disorder.

Borscht

drawing 014 2006
pen and ink 22x17 in

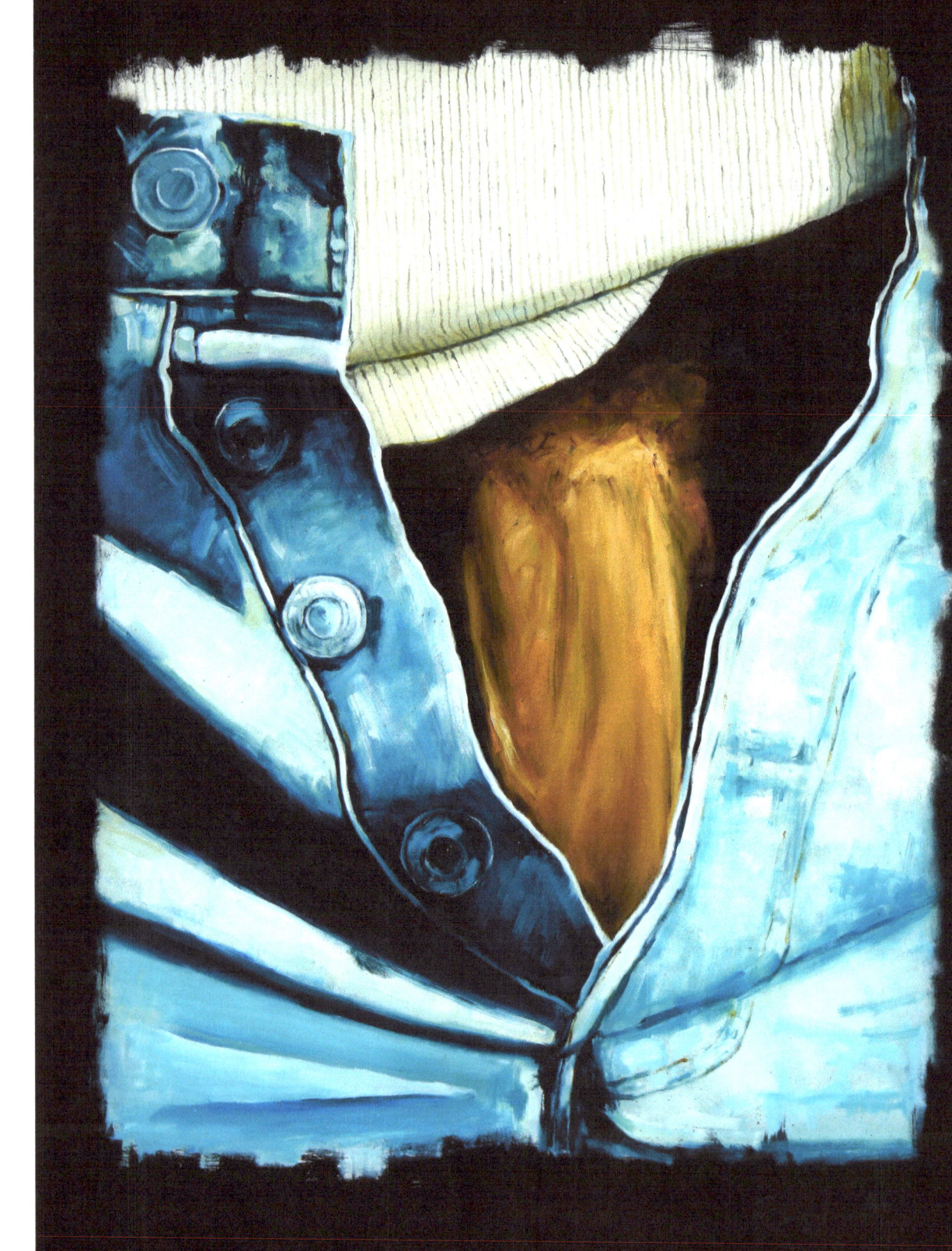

wife beater 2012 »
oil on canvas 48x36 in

Bottomline

The bottom line is this.

I'm a simple country boy from Barnaul Russia, I like things made with taste and passion. I prefer the simpler things in life, like dear friends, good music and food. I love to create, and despite being told I can't, I do. I'm no one special, I'm just me...

Biryukoff

painter, sound artist, performer

2011 Co-founder of the XAR non profit Corporation (eXchange Art Residency) in NJ USA
2010 Release of "Fictive Planets" – sound art collaboration with Ego Ex Nihil from
        Yekaterinburg
2009 Rut – Collaboration with poet Victor Ivaniv from Novosibirsk
2008 Soundtrack for the CGI movie Tamara and Demon
2008 Art Residency at the Fine Arts Work Center, Provincetown, MA USA,
        sponsored by ArtsLink, NYC.
2007 Muhmood sound art project formed – www.muhmood.net
2006 Art Competition "Fresh Wind" prize of the viewers' choice
        at the Barnaul Contemporary Art Competition "Fresh Wind"
2005 one of the nudes went to museumMAN in Liverpool UK
2004 first conceptual project (Naked Loneliness)
2002 UK experience triggered a big change in approach
2001 the Second prize at the annual Altai Region Young Artists Exhibition
2000 graduated from the local Teacher Training Univ.
1999 first solo show
1990 moved to Altai, Russia
1976 born in Frunze, Kyrgyzstan

member of the art union Siberian Masters, member of the Young Artists Union of Altai

>>in collections
works in the private collections in Russia, USA, including Hawaii, Caribbean, UK, Canada,
Germany, France, Finland, Switzerland, Australia.
museumMAN Liverpool, UK
PAAM Provincetown MA, USA
CEC ArtsLink New York, USA

>>publications
The ADVOCATE
Bearflavoured
Saatchi Online Critic's Choice
Art Baby Art

>> solo shows

2009   May-June, Turina Gora Gallery, Barnaul, Russia "American Trip"
2008   November, Fine Arts Work Center, Provincetown, MA USA
2007   December, pavilion of contemporary art Open Sky, Barnaul Russia
        "presence.[exe]"
2006   February, pavilion of contemporary art Open Sky, Barnaul Russia "EVENT"
2004   April, pavilion of contemporary art Open Sky, Barnaul Russia "Naked Loneliness"
2002   May-June, Barnaul State Univ,Barnaul Russia "Space"
2001   August, Barnaul State Univ,Barnaul Russia "Islands in the Ocean"
2001   January - February, Talmenka Regional Museum, Altai Russia "Thirty Impressions"
1999   December, Talmenka Regional Museum, Altai Russia
        "The First Personal Exhibition"

>> other shows

2007   July, Barnaul, Russia Siberia Regional Young Artists Juried Exibition
2007   April - July, The Kinsey Institute Gallery, Bloomington, IN USA
        Juried Erotic Art Show
2007   March, Cedar Rapids, IA USA UNcover Show
2006   March - April, Barnaul, Russia Barnaul
        Contemporary Art Competition Show "Fresh Wind"
2005   October - November, Novosibirsk Russia
        Siberian Masters group exhibition "Wind From The Sea"
2004   June -July, St.Petersburg Russia
        The Second International Biennial of Graphics "White International Nights 2004"
2004   June - Augst, Berdsk Russia Siberian Masters group exhibition
2003   December - 2004 February, Novosibirsk Russia Siberian Masters group exhibition
2003   July, Barnaul Russia Annual Altai Young Artists Juried Exibition
2003   June, Barnaul Russia The first exhibition of the Art Group "FOUR"
2002   August, Barnaul Russia Annual Altai Young Artists Juried Exibition
2001   December - 2002, January, Barnaul Russia
        Ehxibition of Art Union "Vzglyad"- "CARNIVAL"
2001   November,Barnaul Russia "Regional Altai Art Exhibition"
2001   September - October,Barnaul Russia Annual Altai Young Artists Exhibition
2000   December -2001, January, Barnaul Russia
        Ehxibition of Art Union "Vzglyad"- "MILLENIUM"
2000   June, Barnaul Russia Annual Altai Young Artists Juried Exibition

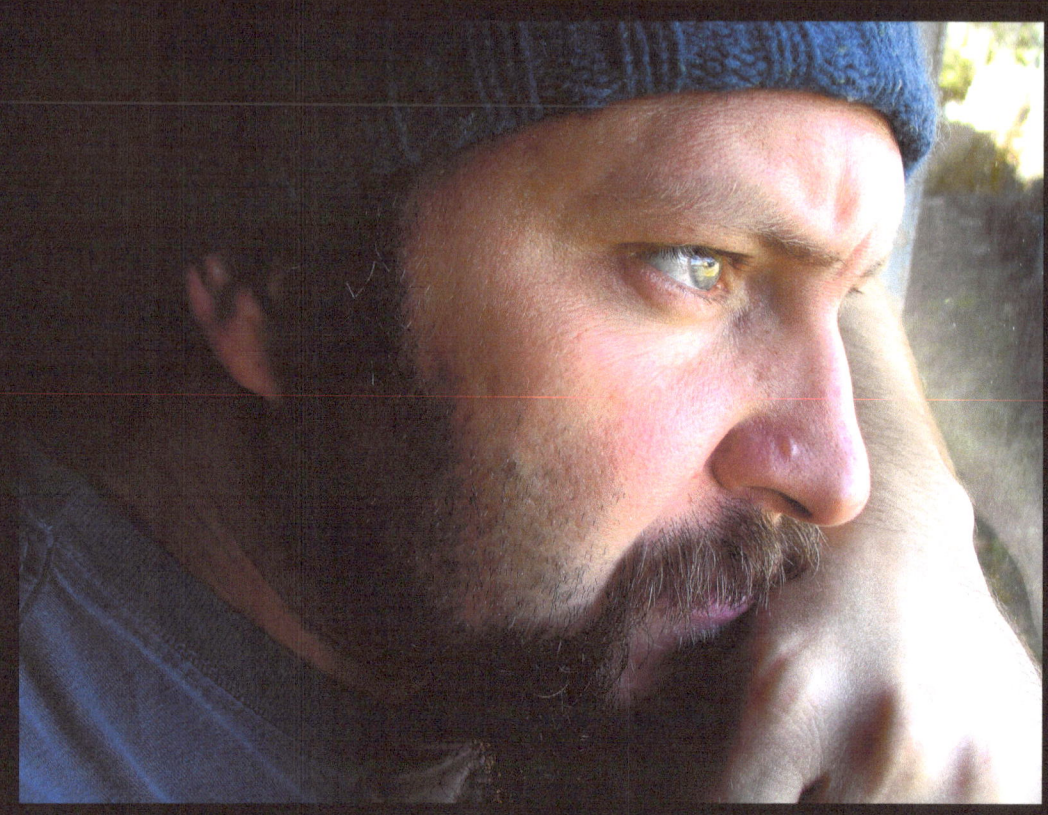

www.biryukoff.com
www.muhmood.net
a@biryukoff.com

a special thank you for a great deal of patience and support to Tom Frank and Albert, without you guys this book would not be possible